This book belongs to

....

Everyone has tonsils, they sit inside your mouth
They squeeze the food and snacks you eat
And tingle when you SHOUT!

Just like squishy little cushions
Far back in your throat
Everybody has them
Even cows and even goats!

Tonsils fight infections
That can leave you feeling bad
But sometimes tonsils get it wrong
And end up getting sad

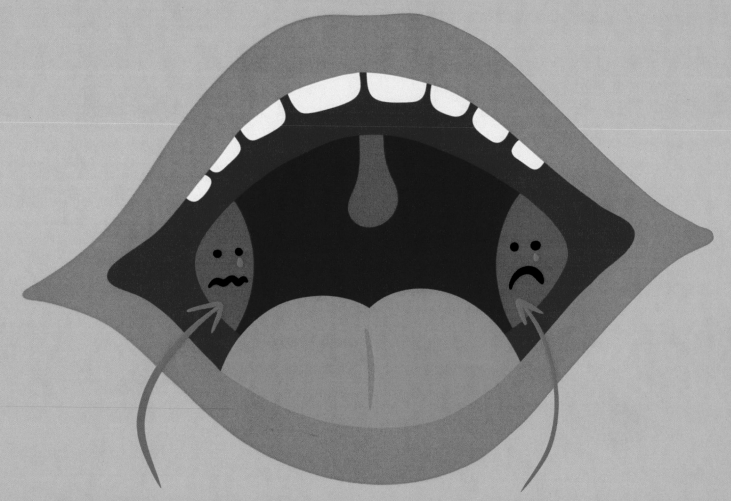

This is where your tonsils are! Can you see them in a mirror?

It might start as a headache
Or feeling kind of sick
Maybe it's a scratchy cough
That medicine can't kick

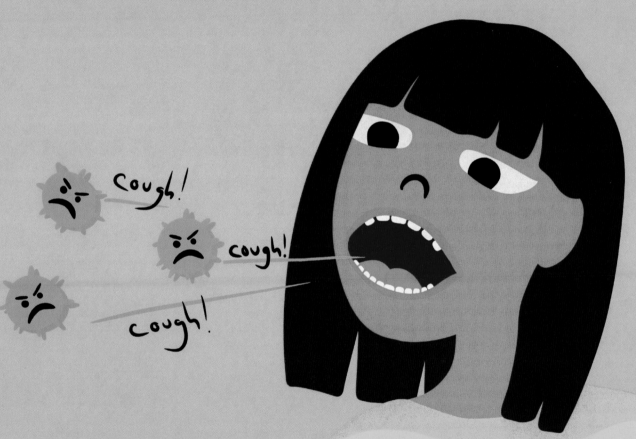

You might have trouble swallowing
Does your throat keep feeling sore?
If that's the case, your tonsils
Just aren't working anymore!

But there's no need to worry
The solution is quite clear
It's easier than jumping jacks
Or whistling out your ear!

A very clever doctor
In their very clever way
Will do some clever things
To take those silly tonsils away

You'll go into the hospital
And lay in a comfy bed
You'll have a snoozy sleep
To rest your poorly little head

And then while you are snoozing
Doctor will look inside your mouth
And with a squeeze and poke and prod
They'll take your tonsils out!

Later when you wake up
Your throat might be quite sore
But then you'll feel your tonsils
Do not hurt you anymore

Have a couple of days of snoozing
And reading in your bed
Eat lots of cold and soft foods
And rest your little head

Then when you're feeling better
You can sing and shout "HOORAY!
MY THROAT IS OH, SO HAPPY
WITH MY TONSILS GONE AWAY!"

Can you name these parts of your mouth?

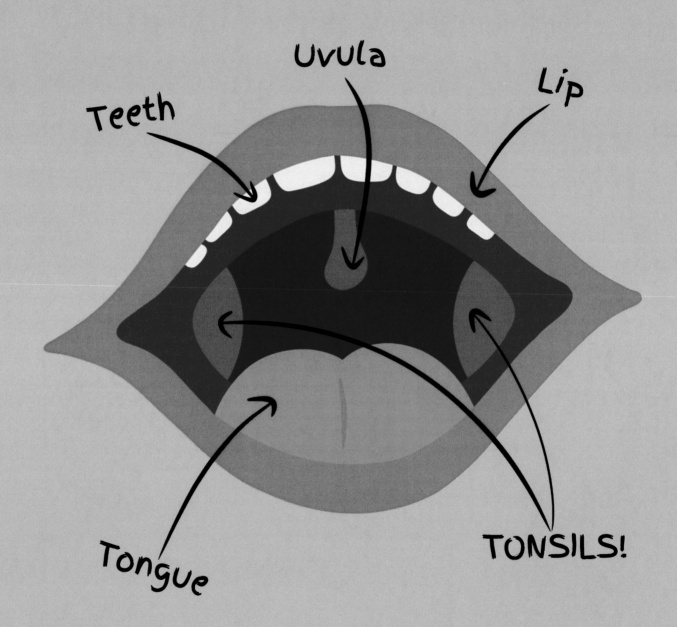

Uvula

Teeth

Lip

Tongue

TONSILS!